"Dave"
A Monarch's Tale

Written and Illustrated by J. R. Ford

Hardcover ISBN: 978-1-7343299-4-0

Paperback ISBN: 978-1-7343299-6-4

Ebook IBSN: 978-1-7343299-5-7

Published by:
Jillybean Creations, LLC
September 2020

Copyright 2020

JillybeanCreationsLLC.com

You may contact the publisher at
JillybeanCreationsllc.com
or by sending an email to :

JillybeanPublishing@gmail.com

"Dave"
A Monarch's Tale

~ Written and Illustrated by ~
J.R. Ford

This story was inspired by the
migrating Monarch's
at
Pickerel Lake State Campground
Vanderbilt, MI
and
my friend Dave.

PICKEREL LAKE
STATE CAMPGROUND

Hi, I am Dave,

and this is the story of my life

...so far!

I ... am a Caterpillar...no really, I am.

Do you see that handsome guy over there on that

milkweed plant, that's me.

But I was not always this good looking.

I was once a tiny egg attached to the bottom
of a milkweed leaf!

It took me four whole days to wiggle out of
my egg.

Once I was out, I was very hungry,
so I started eating the milkweed leaf!

Milkweed ~ *The monarch caterpillar is born on the underside of a milkweed leaf and this is the only plant it will eat.*

After two or three days I will shed my skin, (molt),

and after my second molt,

I get my COOL stripes.

Every time I need to grow, I will molt.

It seems like this happens about every
three days.

Now I am getting big and plump!

So far, my life has been pretty boring,

just eating all day long…

…the only thing that ever changes is

seeing another caterpillar,

I call him Danny…that is him over there with Carol,

the ladybug…

Hi Danny! Hi Carol!

They never answer…or wave!

Probably because they do not have any hands,

just legs!

Other than seeing Danny and Carol...
I sometimes see that pretty colored bird over there and
those bees gathering nectar and pollen.

The nectar in all milkweed flowers provides valuable food for
butterflies, bees, and other pollinators, including this
Ruby Throated Hummingbird.

The milkweed plant has a toxin in it.
We eat it and have the toxin in us.
This means that our predators will die if they eat us.

It has been about two weeks, I am looking good and now I am full grown.

I have been feeling like I want to make something…
I just do not know what it is I am supposed to make!

Let me think about it as I sleep tonight, maybe something will come to mind . . . zzzZZZ!

When I woke up this morning, I felt something on my
mouth, so I did what any caterpillar would do,
I grabbed it with my **true legs**
(Those are my front six legs) …

…I keep pulling and pulling, but it does not
end, I try to wipe it off on a leaf and it sticks to the
leaf like a button…

…now I have this sticky stuff (silk) on my
true legs, my mouth and the leaf.
I am just hanging here by silk and this spiky thing
called a **cremaster** and I cannot move!

I am trying to get comfortable by moving some things
around inside my body a bit.

I shed my outer skin (exoskeleton).

I feel like I could sleep for ten days straight!

The caterpillar will molt one last time becoming a **Chrysalis**.
This is where the metamorphosis begins.

Metamorphosis ~ *the process of transformation from an immature form (larvae) to an adult form (butterfly) in two or more distinct stages.*

I am having this dream...like I am inside a sleeping bag

with the zipper stuck...

...when all of the sudden I wake up and go to stretch...

and ... **WHOA**...Wait a minute ...
something is not right here, where is
my handsome pinstriped body?

I have turned into ...a **Butterfly!**

Look at me, I have legs and I have wings ...

I HAVE WINGS!

How **COOL** is that!

I CAN FLY!

Bye, Bye Milkweed, I need some sweet Nectar!

...WOW...

look at all those flowers over there!

They are so colorful, and I am very hungry for some
nectar...

Nectar ~ a sugary fluid secreted by plants, especially within
flowers to encourage pollination by insects and other animals.
It is collected by bees to make into honey.

I have been flying all around the fields for about six
weeks now, enjoying the sun and nectar from
all the beautiful flowers…

…new ones seem to pop up every few days.

OH, WOW!

Look at all of those golden colored flowers over there
across the road…

I will just fly over there and check them out…

…the meadow is beautiful and some of the other butterflies told me the flowers are called Goldenrod flowers.

flippity flap...

flappity ... flip

all this flippity flapping is making me quite thirsty,
maybe there is some water up ahead past
these trees.

It seems I cannot fly in a straight line, so it is taking a
bit longer for me to get there because I am all over the
place flappity flipping these wings.

Oh, look over there, a lake and more butterflies
like me…

...I do need to rest a bit, maybe I will land on
that thing in the lake for a few minutes to
catch my breath.

I see all the butterflies flying around by the
shore where all the flowers are.
There sure are a lot of them over there, maybe
I can meet some new friends!

I met three guys hanging out on some goldenrod…
Lester, Terry, and George.
They told me it is time for our migration.

They are getting ready to fly south for warmer weather
and that is what I am supposed to do.

We are heading for a place called
Sierra Madre del Sur,
a mountain range in southern Mexico.

Well, now that we all have filled up on nectar, we have quite a journey ahead of us.

The weather is starting to change here so we are off to find the warmer weather.

WOW... there are hundreds of us all flying at the same time!

Monarchs *will fly 30-50 miles a day during winter migration and have been known to fly up to 4,000 miles in its lifetime. They rest several times during the day to eat nectar and roost at night in trees before continuing on their journey.*

Now that we have reached Mexico, we will stay here
for about six months soaking up the
sun's rays…

…and hopefully, I will find a mate and the monarch life
cylce will start again.

I just remembered; I need to send Danny a
post card….

That is my adventure ....

as told by me,

Dave!

The **Monarch Butterfly** life cycle is the **egg**, the **larvae** (caterpillar), the **pupa** (chrysalis), and the **adult butterfly**.

In March and April generation one will be born, May and June generation two, July and August generation three and September and October generation four.

Butterfly Friendly Plants - Coneflowers, Zinnias, Porter weed, Butterfly Bush, Cosmic Cosmos, Mexican Sunflower, Summer Beauty Allium, Goldenrod, Lantana, Lilac and Ironweed.

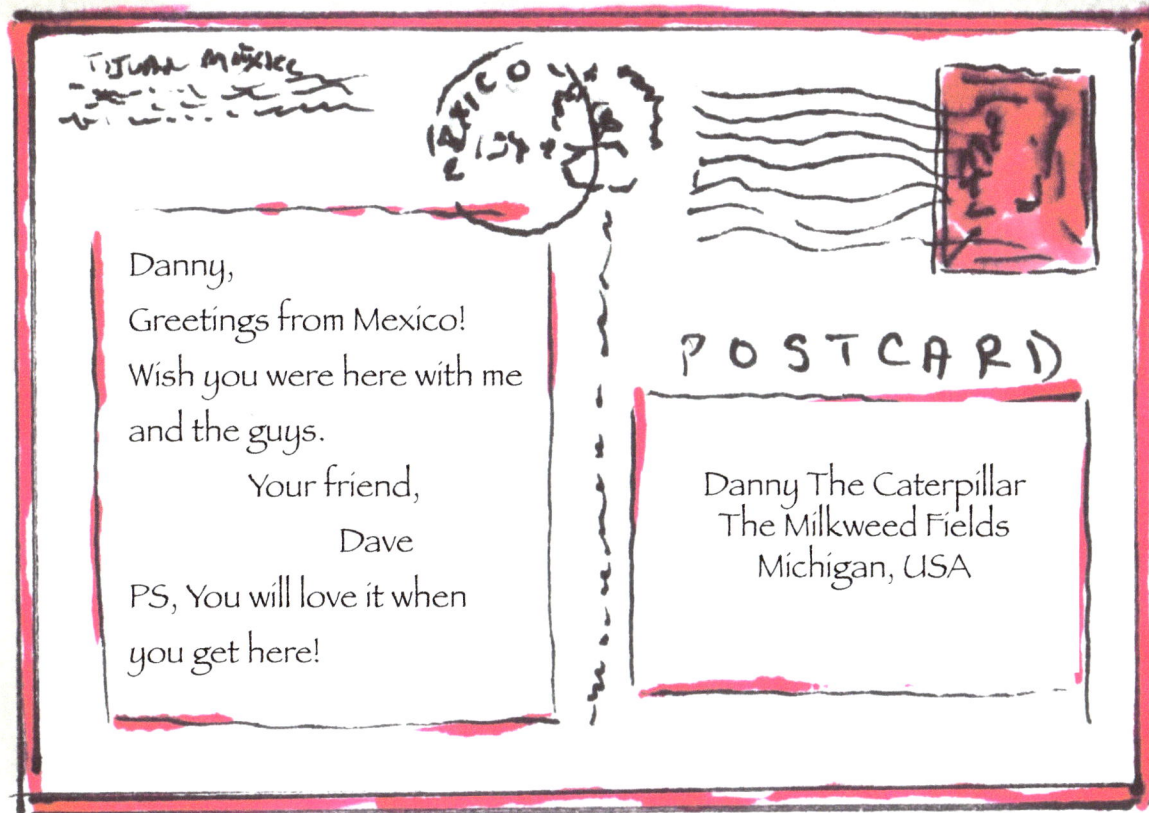

Danny,
Greetings from Mexico!
Wish you were here with me
and the guys.
        Your friend,
            Dave
PS, You will love it when
you get here!

POSTCARD

Danny The Caterpillar
The Milkweed Fields
Michigan, USA

The End!

If you enjoyed reading about Dave please leave a review on our website:

JillybeanCreationsLLC.com.

Thank You!

USAF VETERAN WRITER

www.ingramcontent.com/pod-product-compliance
Lightning Source LLC
Chambersburg PA
CBHW060825270326
41931CB00002B/61

9 781734 329964